Chad the Cherry's Charming and Cheeky Chalkboard Chants

EILEEN DISTASIO-CLARK

With Great Love and Appreciation to Those Who Have and Do Bless My Life.

My Family:

Joseph DeStasio Sr. & Miriam Lucille Baragone DeStasio, My Late Parents.

Andrea Jean DeStasio McIntosh, My Older Sister and Their Families.

Joseph DeStasio Jr., My Younger and Only Brother and Their Families.

Donna Marie DeStasio Wagner, My Younger Sister and Their Families.

My Children:

Eileen, Rebekah, Rachel, S. Michael,

Jennifer, Sharon, Tara, Stephanie,

Apryll, Mikaelah, & M. Trevor

and THEIR Families!!

ACKNOWLEDGMENTS

First and foremost, I express, deeply, my sincere gratitude to our Heavenly Father for blessing me with the gift and talent of writing! I know I could not do what I do without His assistance.

I also want to acknowledge and express gratitude to my children, Eileen, Rebekah, Rachel, S. Michael, Jennifer, Sharon, Tara, Stephanie, Apryll, Mikaelah, and M. Trevor, who were very active in 'creating' many tales about the Hunk-a-Doodles.

Truth be told, I really do not know how we came up with the name, Hunk-a-Doodles, but I give the credit for that to my children. I must also credit them for the inspirations that produced these stories because it was through their sweet and innocent childhood antics that they were originally originated!

INTRODUCTION

In 1992, shortly after my family moved to Missouri, I found, in a Clearance Sale Bin in the Hy-Vee grocery store, five stuffed fruits: a cherry, a lemon, an orange, a plum, and a watermelon. They were so cute I just had to buy them!

Once home, I put them on the half wall that separated the kitchen from the living room, where they sat for the whole time that we lived in that house. Now, of course, any time we had to move, they did too. We loved them too much to leave them behind!

In different homes, they usually sat in different places, on the wall above the stairs, on a bed, usually mine, on the back of the couch, on... well, just wherever we wanted them to sit. But sitting was not all that they did.

We played with them, we used them to decorate for special occasions, we... well, we just had a great deal of fun with them!

We called them our Hunk-a-Doodles, but I really do not recall how we came up with that name. We also gave each one of them their own name. The cherry was identified as Chad, the orange was named Ollie, the lemon was called Larry, the plum was Peter, and the watermelon was given the name Wally!

We also made up fun stories with them and that is what motivated me to write these stories to share with you! So, please read and enjoy them, over and over and over again!

CHAD THE CHERRY'S CHARMING AND CHEEKY CHALKBOARD CHANTS

It was a quiet day, a rainy day, a day to stay inside.

But what to do, wondered Chad the Cherry, since he no longer had to hide.

'Wait!' I think you are thinking, 'Why would he have to hide just because it was raining?'

Well, remember, the Hunk-a-Doodles used to sit on the Lofty-White-Wall. So, when it rained, they always had to climb off the wall and go 'hide' under the trees in the Welcoming Woods. But now that they had a home, they did not have to do that. So, when it rained, Chad...

Wait a minute. Rather than me just telling you what he did when it rained, let us go back to where we were before I brought you here so you can see what he did.

Ready? You are?! Great! Let us be going.

"I know!" he said to himself, "What I will do on this rainy day?"

3

Then to the big kitchen chalkboard he went, where he began to write away.

First, he picked up the piece of red chalk, 'cause that color he liked best.

Then began to write what he had earlier thought while he had been taking a rest.

He wrote and wrote and wrote and wrote until he was finally done.

But then, of course he did not stop right there because writing was so much fun!

So, he picked up the orange chalk and began to write some more.

He wrote and he wrote, he wrote and wrote 'till Larry came through the door.

After a nice greeting, Larry sat down with a puzzle to do.

Then Chad chose the yellow and purple chalk to write another chant or two.

Now because he liked diversity, when he was finished with those,

He put down the purple chalk he had just used, and green was the next one he chose.

About the time Chad finished that chant, in came the other three Hunks.

Now, he might have started another one, but he knew it was time for chunks.

"Uhhhhh, what are chunks?" You are probably asking. So, I will tell you. To the Hunks, chunks are meals. Therefore, when Ollie, Peter, and Wally came into the kitchen, both Chad and Larry quickly finished what they were doing so they could help make their supper.

As Larry put his puzzle, which he had finished just before Ollie, Peter, and Wally had come into the kitchen, back into its box, and Chad put down his chalk and washed his hands, Peter and Ollie were discussing what they should make for dinner. But, to all of their surprise, well all except Wally, as Wally told them that they did not have to make dinner; they just needed to get things ready by setting the table for six—not just five—diners, and wait for ReFinjen to arrive. He then explained to them why.

"Just in case you do not remember, I will be happy to tell you.

"We are not making dinner tonight 'cause that, ReFinjen will do.

"We saw her when we were out yesterday, when we all were taking a walk.

"We stopped and chatted 'bout this and that, and this is what came from that talk.

"ReFinjen said she missed seeing us and wanted to come for a visit,

"And we told her we loved that idea, that none of us would miss it.

"She also said—and we liked what she said—and this is was that was.

"She said, for us, dinner she would make and her reason was, "Just because."

Well, after a chorus of "Oh yeah! I remember now!" They all worked together, as they always did. Wiped off the table, covered it with their favorite tablecloth, got out the plates, utensils, glasses, and napkins and laid them out on the sides of the table for six—not just five—diners. Then, in the middle of the table, though they did not know what they would be eating, they put the salt and pepper shakers, and a pitcher—a big pitcher—of iced cold water. At exactly the time they were done and had just placed the last piece of dinnerware on the table, they heard a knock on the door, and sure enough, it was ReFinjen!

They greeted her warmly, as always they did when anyone came to their home. They invited her in and helped her arrange the food on the table. Well, actually, they arranged it on each one's plate, since ReFinjen had made for each of them what she had learned was their favorite dinner food! Now, because I think I am right to think that you are wondering what that was, I will tell you.

For Chad and Peter, who like pretty much the same things, she brought sun-baked seeds. For Ollie, who tends to be a little picky, she brought water-boiled pits. For Larry, who would really rather not eat, she brought lightly seasoned rinds. For Wally, who likes everything, she brought lightly seasoned, boiled

8

in water seeded pits, and sun-baked rinds. And, for herself she brought a bowl of lettuce and tomato salad.

Once the plates were all filled and the water was poured into the glasses, with everyone sitting on their seats, and the prayer having been said, they all began eating. And boy, did they love it!! They complimented and thanked ReFinjen over and over and over again. And she thanked them equally as much for what she considered to be a blessed opportunity to serve them and spend some time with them. And while they were spending that time together, they had a great conversation about what everyone had done that day.

Since ReFinjen, even though she had been the one to prepare the meal, was considered the guest, upon the Hunks' request, she went first.

"Well," she began, "I got up early and went out to gather all the stuff I needed to make this dinner for you. It was so much fun! I never shopped this way before and I really enjoyed it! Then, when I got home, I had to look up some recipes for this stuff because I never made anything like this before, and I found it all very interesting. After that, I took a walk, I do that every day, and when I got back home, I did my chores, packed our dinner in a box and hurried over here!"

Wally was the next one to share his adventures. Well, it was actually Wally and Ollie who shared their adventures because they had done what they had done together, and this is what they had done.

"Oh, it was awesome!" Wally stated energetically.

"Yeah! No kidding," Ollie chimed in. "I loved climbing the Catalpa tree!"

"And," Wally added, "we got to the very top."

"Where we found a ring in a nest," Ollie said, "when for a rest we did stop!"

Then, before moving on to the next story, Ollie ran and got the ring, showed it to everyone and let them try it on, if they wanted to, but only ReFinjen could. Then it was Peter's turn to tell about his day.

"Wow, that is super awesome," Peter excitedly commented.

Then he added, "I tried to drive a car, but its back bumper I dented.

"But think not that I was careless, it was really not my fault;

"It was the Lofty White Wall that brough me to a halt!"

Now, of course, that comment brought on a stadium sized volume of laughter from all five of the Hunks and ReFinjen. When they were finally able to gain control of themselves, Larry was the one who spoke up and said:

"Well, I really did not do much today,

"Most of the time, in my room I day stay.

"But later, not too long ago,

"I worked on a puzzle. I love them, you know!"

Yes, that was something everyone did know, and they also knew that he was quite good at puzzling, in many ways, actually.

Then Chad ended the daily reports with this:

"Well, I did what I always do when I do what I like best.

"I wrote, and wrote and wrote, until I needed a rest.

"And that was when you all came in, well Larry was already here,

"So, we could eat our dinner and our activities share and cheer!

Now, that comment sparked a whole new conversation!

"What did you write?" Ollie asked.

"Is that what is on the board?" Peter wanted to know.

"Yeah," Larry said, "with that himself he tasked."

"Well," Wally questioned, "will you read them to us, or no?"

"Yeah, do that please," ReFinjen agreed.

"I would really love to hear you read.

"What you wrote on your board today.

"I have heard that wonderful things you say!"

"Of course, I will!" Chad confirmed.

As up, he got from the table.

"As soon as I finish washing my plate,

"I will be ready and able."

After everyone finished their dinner, washed their plates and put them away, and straightened up the kitchen, they set up their chairs in front of the chalkboard. Now, because Chad had decided that, rather than having Ollie, Larry, Peter, Wally, and ReFinjen just listen to all of the chants, he would have each of them read one, so, he asked them to sit in the order in which they would be reading. Then he explained:

"I will read the red," Chad said, "because that matches me.

"Ollie, you read the orange because that looks like you.

"Larry, take the yellow, since the yellow chant matches thee,

"And Peter, read the purple, since you are purple too.

"Then Wally, you read the next one, the one that is green,

"Because that one, as you know, is the color of you.

"Then ReFinjen, the last one will be yours to read.

"That is what I think is the way, this we should do."

Now, since all of them liked that idea, that is what they did!

Chad, stood in front of the chalkboard, on the far-left side of the board where he had written the red chant, cleared his throat, and read:

"Chad's Charming Red Chant"

"Red! Red! Red! You may have heard it said.

"Red! Red! Red! With Knowledge you are fed.

"Red! Red! Red! Keeps you from the bed.

"Red! Red! Red! Good Health from feet to head.

"Red! Red! Red! Power, Passion, Vitality, and the Spirit.

"Red! Red! Red! Redeeming, Sacrifice, always Aware of it.

"Red! Red! Red! Individual Worth.

"Red! Red! Red! You have a place on Earth!"

After Chad finished reading, with everyone in thoughtful silence, Ollie got up, went to the chalkboard and read:

"Chad's Charming Orange Chant"

"Orange! Orange! Orange! Choices will help you change.

"Orange! Orange! Orange! Creativity can rearrange.

"Orange! Orange! Orange! Service is not strange.

"Orange! Orange! Orange! Energetically arrange.

"Orange! Orange! Orange! Compassion is not a challenge.

"Orange! Orange! Orange! Accountability has vast range.

"Orange! Orange! Orange! From worldliness does estrange.

"Orange! Orange! Orange! With Joy, sadness can exchange."

When Ollie finished reading, with everyone still in quiet awe, Larry proceeded to the chalkboard and read:

"Chad's Charming Yellow Chant"

"Yellow! Yellow! Yellow! Good Works their Virtue bellow.

"Yellow! Yellow! Yellow! Loyal and Friendly is every good fellow.

"Yellow! Yellow! Yellow! Right Knowledge is strong and mellow.

"Yellow! Yellow! Yellow! Happiness is a constant hello.

"Yellow! Yellow! Yellow! Intelligence sings out like a cello.

"Yellow! Yellow! Yellow! Hope makes one sweet as Jello.

"Yellow! Yellow! Yellow! Optimism is so far up from below.

"Yellow! Yellow! Yellow! Joy comes from Heaven's Meadow."

It was rather obvious that all of the Hunk-a-Doodles, and their friend were deep in thought as each of the Chants were read. And that was no surprise because, truth be told, the chants were quite thought-provoking. So, of course, when one was reading, the others were deeply thinking about what was being read.

No! Wait a minute! Let me correct that!

When one was reading, all of them were deeply thinking about what was being read. After all, whoever was reading was also thinking about what was being read. Now, moving on.

With silence setting the stage, and no need for any promptings, Peter, went to the chalkboard, stood in front of the Purple Chant, which was just to the right of the Yellow Chant, and read:

"Chad's Charming Purple Chant"

"Purple! Purple! Purple! With Faith we will rise over every hurdle.

"Purple! Purple! Purple! Spiritual Growth, us will encircle.

"Purple! Purple! Purple! Transformation, from us, will burgle.

"Purple! Purple! Purple! Puts us in a Wisdom circle.

"Purple! Purple! Purple! Integrity must be universal.

"Purple! Purple! Purple! The greatest type of Wealth is internal.

"Purple! Purple! Purple! Service in Abundance, to us, speaks Paternal.

"Purple! Purple! Purple! Seeing all Beauty, to us, speaks Maternal."

When Peter finished reading the Purple Chant, the silence in the room was even more silent. So, as Peter sat down, Wally got up and quietly walked to the chalkboard where the Green Chant was written and read:

"Chad's Charming Green Chant"

"Green! Green! Green! Growing Spirituality is really keen.

18

"Green! Green! Green! Gaining Greater Knowledge is what that will mean.

"Green! Green! Green! With Love, toward Heaven, we must always lean.

"Green! Green! Green! Through Faith, Proper Prosperity we will redeem.

"Green! Green! Green! Beauty and Renewal like no one has seen.

"Green! Green! Green! In Harmony with Heaven, from the world we will wean.

"Green! Green! Green! Hope will abound, like never there has been.

"Green! Green! Green! Peace will be the setting of every scene."

Finally, with reverence and awe, ReFinjen got up, walked quietly to the right side of the chalkboard and read the last chant:

Chad's Fabulous Friends Chant

"Friends! Friends! Friends! To have, are oh so good!

"Friends! Friends! Friends! Get together when we could!

"Friends! Friends! Friends! Help us do what we should!

"Friends! Friends! Friends! Keep us strong, like cebil wood!

"Friends! Friends! Friends! Do not create falsehood!

"Friends! Friends! Friends! With love, cover us like a hood!

"Friends! Friends! Friends! We are always understood!

"Friends! Friends! Friends! They make us feel so good!"

Well, needless to say, but I will say it anyway, when ReFinjen was done, she quietly went back to her chair and sat as still as all the Hunks were sitting. They all were pretty certain that they all knew that they all were thinking the same thing. And what that was, was this.

Chad had always written chants on the chalkboard, ever since Rovert and LeChar found their house for them, and Eniele and Lalpry bought the chalkboard and put it up in their kitchen. They had thought it would be a good place to write notes to each other and jot down things they needed to remember to do. But Chad turned it into his Chalkboard Chants Board!

Now, writing chants was just one of the many crazy things that Chad loved to do, and he did it very well! But until this time, Chad's Chants had always been kind of cheeky. But this time his chants were quite different. They were... well... charming and... hmmmm... they were inspirational. Now, it was not that Chad was not spiritual; he definitely was. They all were. It was just that he had never written chants like these before. So, as everyone quietly sat, they also thought. They wanted to know why these chants were so different.

So, after a little bit of a bit of a while, Larry asked:

"Chad, what made you write your chants this way?

"They are really cool and great to read,

"But most of the time, they are cheeky, indeed!

"So, why did you write differently today?"

"Well, a couple of days ago, when I was working in the garden,

"I was thinking about all our friends, and how their hearts they never harden.

"I thought about Rovert and LeChar, HaKeber and Eniele,

"I thought about Einahpets, LeAchim, Norash, and Lalpry.

"I thought about ReFinjen, Haleakim, and Rata,

"And thought that thank them again, we oughta."

"I thought about all the things they did for us,

"Like finding us a house and making it a home

"So, we could live nicely and never have to roam.

"I thought about how they do such good, and never make a fuss."

"That was when I decided that I wanted to write

"About the things that—without words—they taught,

"How kind and good—to be—we aught,

"Just by being what they are, how they act day and night."

After a tiny moment of quiet contemplation, ReFinjen said, "Chad, that is really sweet, and I would be very happy to help you do that for all the others."

Then before Chad, or any of the Hunks could say anything, she continued with, "We really are all friends, and they have helped me too. So, I would love to help you express thanks to all of them. And, if you insist, I would be happy to receive a gift from you!"

After that, she went on to say, "I think we should copy these chants on stone. We could paint them on big, flat, smooth stones, like the ones all over the ground in Welcoming Woods. And then, when they are ready, I would be very happy to help you deliver them. And I would be very grateful to hang one in my home too!"

Now, it was no surprise that Chad most definitely loved that idea. And, truth be told, Ollie, Larry, Peter, and Wally did too! So, sooner than soon, like that very same day, or should I say evening, they began their search for the stone.

They searched and hunted and hunted and searched until they found the perfect stones, on which they painted Chad's Charming Chalkboard Chants. They painted one for each of themselves, the chant that had been written for them, and Chad's Fabulous Friends Chant on a dozen more stones.

However, because they had found so many more stones than that, they also painted also painted some of Chad's Cheeky Chalkboard Chants. Now, because we, that is Me and all the Hunks, think you might like to know what those Cheeky Chants are, we will share them with you too.

Chad's Cheeky, Red Chant

Apples with dapples, and Pumpkin Pie, taste so good
they make me cry.

I really, really do not know why, but they taste so
good, I want to fly.

Chad's Cheeky Orange Chant

Tiger Lillies are oh-so cool. Monarch Butterflies are
like a tool!

But what I never learned in school, was that for the
Monarch the Tiger is a stool.

Chad's Cheeky Yellow Chant

He is a yellow, mellow, fellow, who really likes to
bellow.

With a mouth full of his Jello, is how he says hello!

Chad's Cheeky Purple Chant

Squash me, I dare you, before I count to two.

But just know that if you do, I will scare you with
Boo Hoo!

Chad's Cheeky Green Chant

Goo Goo was hosing down a path, until a spook said,
"Give me all you hath."

Well, after doing all the math, what he gave him
was a bath.

Okay, so now that you know what the Hunk-a-
Doodles put together for all of their friends, would you
like to go with us to deliver them? You would! Great!!
Then let us be going.

It was on a bright Saturday morning, when the
Hunks packed one each of the Charming Chants and
the Cheeky Chants into eleven different bags. Then,
because, truth be told, they did not know where all
their friends lived, they headed out to Fiddle-Faddle
Park, the playground park that was in the middle of
town. They were certain they would find them, or at
least most of them, there because they knew that they
all loved to play on the swings and the slides, the
monkey bars and the merry-go-rounds, the... well, you
get the idea. Anyway, with all the bags in hand, well
hands, off to Fiddle-Faddle Park they went. And when
they got there, they did indeed see all of their friends!

Some were playing on the swings, and others were
climbing the rock walls. Still others were sliding down
the sliding boards while others were going up and
down on the see-saws.

"Hey, everyone," ReFinjen called as she jumped down from the top of the rock wall. "I see the Hunk-a-Doodles."

"Really?" Lalpry questioned, as she jumped off the swing. "Where are they?"

Looking in the direction to which ReFinjen was pointing, which was across the baseball field, Lalpry and everyone else did see the Hunks. So happy was everyone to see the Hunks at the park that had never happened before, that they ran to meet them. As they ran to meet the Hunks, the Hunks ran to meet them. And it did not take long for them to meet each other just a few feet from where ReFinjen had first seen the Hunks.

"Huh?" You are saying, "How could that be?"

Well, remember, the Hunks are quite small and they have very little feet, with no legs. Or do they have little legs with no feet? Well, whatever the case is, they could not run very fast, in fact, we probably cannot call what they did running. So, yes, all the L.D.S got to them before they had gotten very far at all.

"Hi, guys!" came eleven shouts, loud and strong!

"Hello, Sises and Bros!" called Chad the Cherry.

"Yo! We are so glad to see, so Howdy!" chimed Ollie the Orange.

"Hi, glad you are here when we came by!" Larry said.

"Hey, finding you made my day!" shouted Peter.

"Glad we blew in; wanna know what we are doin'!" Wally called out.

"We are having a great time," ReFinjen responded energetically. "And we are feeling even better now that you are all here."

"Well," Wally began, "we were pretty sure that you all would be."

"And," Larry said, "you are the ones we wanted to see."

"So," Chad continued, "we decided to come by."

"So, we could see you and say Hi!" Ollie stated.

"Because," Peter explained, "we have something for all of you, so find you, was what we needed to do."

"You have something for us?" Lalpry questioned curiously.

"What is it?" LeChar asked with equal curiosity.

That was when the Hunks handed a bag of stones to each of their friends and together explained:

"Well, we have something for you, because we love you so!

"And how much you mean to us, is something we want you to know!

"That is why we came here today; we knew this is where we could find you!

"For you, these are, so you will know how grateful we are for all that you do!"

As Eniele, HaKeber, LeChar, LeAchim, ReFinjen, Norash, Rata, Einahpets, Lalpry, Haleakim, and Rovert took the stones out of the bags and read what was on them, their expressions changed from inquisitive stares to full smiles of genuine joy and appreciation.

After looking at each other, as if for a cue, all the friends said, in unison, "Oh, my goodness! These are so beautiful! You guys are so sweet! I love these!"

Then, as they sat together on the grass at the far end of the baseball field, Chad, Ollie, Larry, Peter, and Wally explained why they had decided to paint Chad's Chants on the stones and give them to them.

"You have been so good to us," Chad began.

"You have taught so much to us," Ollie continued.

"You have been best friends to us," Larry added.

"You have shown what really good friends mean to us," Peter explained.

"You are the greatest friends anyone has ever been to us," Wally concluded.

Then, in unison, all the Hunks also said:

"You have taken care of us!

"You taught and helped, gave and served.

"You never got mad when we made a fuss!

"You comforted calmly and never came unnerved.

"You are what we have always needed,

"And more than what we craved.

"From us sadness and sorrow you weeded,

"And from loneliness, us, you saved."

Of course, a round of hugs, genuine and sincere, were shared by everyone, with everyone. And then, again with everyone looking at each other, knowing what each other was thinking, in unison, as they looked at all the Hunk-a-Doodles: Chad the Cherry, Ollie the Orange, Larry the Lemon, Peter the Plum, and Wally the Watermelon, they said, "Well, after all, that is what families do. And we are all family!!"

The End...

Or is it the,

Another Step?

ABOUT THE AUTHOR

Eileen DiStasio-Clark is the second oldest of four children. She is the mother of eleven children and grandmother to twenty-three grandchildren, to date. As a member of The Church of Jesus Christ of Latter-Day Saints, she serves in various positions, teaching, leading, and ministering to children, youth, and adults. Currently, she is also a Family History Missionary. Eileen established the Pursuit of Excellence Institute of Family Education, a non-profit organization focused on strengthening the family. Presently she holds an A.A., a B.A., and an M.A. in Clinical Psychology and is working on the completion of her Doctoral Degree.

Milton Keynes UK
Ingram Content Group UK Ltd.
UKHW051710211124
451363UK00030B/407

9 798330 546824